CELEBRITY BIOS

Jessica Alba

Ursula Rivera

Children's Press®
A Division of Scholastic Inc.
New York / Toronto / London / Auckland / Sydney
Mexico City / New Delhi / Hong Kong
Danbury, Connecticut

Book Design: Michael DeLisio
Contributing Editor: Eric Fein

Photo Credits: Cover © Paul Skipper/Globe Photos; pp. 4, 30 © Fitzroy Barrett/Globe Photos; pp. 6, 9, 10, 12, 15, 24, 27 © The Everett Collection; p. 16 © Rufus F. Folkks/Corbis; pp. 19, 20, 29, 33, 36 © Reuters NewMedia Inc./Corbis; pp. 23, 38 © Tom Rodriguez/Globe Photos; p. 34 © Lisa Rose/Globe Photos

Library of Congress Cataloging-in-Publication Data

Alba, Jessica.
Jessica Alba / by Ursula Rivera.
    p. cm. -- (Celebrity bios)
Includes index.
Summary: Profiles the actress who, at the age of nineteen, became the star of the award-winning television series, "Dark Angel."
    ISBN 0-516-23909-0 (lib. bdg.) -- ISBN 0-516-23482-X (pbk.)
    1. Alba, Jessica, 1981---Juvenile literature. 2. Actors--United States-- Biography--Juvenile literature. [1. Alba, Jessica, 1981– 2. Actors and actresses. 3. Women--Biography.] I. Title. II. Series.

PN2287 .A448 R58 2002
791.45'028'092--dc21
[B]

                                        2001042353

CONTENTS

CHAPTER ONE

Determination

"It was an eye opener. Out here, everyone just wants you to be natural, natural, natural. There's no emphasis on training. But only a very few actors are naturals. You have to study. It's not enough to be cute."

—Jessica in
The New York Times Magazine on the
importance of training for actors

Jessica Alba is one of the hottest young stars in TV and film today. Her stardom is the result of years of hard work. Now, she is a household name. Jessica is a young woman who is not afraid to speak her mind, work hard, and follow her dreams.

Jessica has worked hard all of her life to become the successful actor that she is today.

Jessica's parents, Mark and Cathy, are very
supportive of Jessica's desire to act.

THE EARLY YEARS

Jessica Marie Alba was born on April 28, 1981,
in Pomona, California. Jessica's parents are
Mark and Cathy Alba. Jessica has a mixed ethnic
background. Her father is Mexican-American.
Her mother is Danish and French-Canadian.

Mark Alba was a sergeant in the U.S. Air
Force. When Jessica was a baby, her father was
moved to a military base in Biloxi, Mississippi.
Jessica's brother, Josh, was born there about a
year later.

Determination

The move to Biloxi was the first of many for young Jessica. Each time that Mark was sent to a new base, the family had to relocate. All of the traveling and living in new cities turned out to be good practice for Jessica. As an actor, she would have to spend many weeks working on location, away from home.

Did you know? Jessica is not the only star in the family. Her cousin, Steve Alba, was a skateboarding champ in the late 1970s and '80s.

Growing up, Jessica was like most other girls her age. She attended school and spent time with her friends. Jessica also enjoyed playing sports. She was interested in acting, too. At the age of five, she told her mother she wanted to be an actor.

A YOUNG WINNER

It was several years before Jessica actually tried performing. When she was twelve years old, Jessica and her family were living in Claremont, California. She asked her mother to drive her to an acting competition in nearby Beverly Hills. The grand prize was acting lessons with a professional acting coach. To everyone's surprise, Jessica won the contest!

Jessica learned a lot from the acting lessons. Within a year, she was signed by an agent. Jessica's agent sent her on auditions, or tryouts, for television commercials. Before long, she was a working actor.

Jessica got a small role in the film *Camp Nowhere*. The film starred Jonathan Jackson, who played Lucky Spencer on "General Hospital." Jessica also appeared in commercials for J.C. Penney and Nintendo. Her work was beginning to get noticed by casting agents and television producers.

Jessica's charming personality and determination have helped her become a star.

Jessica (far right) spent two years in Australia filming the TV series "Flipper."

TUNING IN

Jessica's first television role was in "The Secret World of Alex Mack" in 1994. The show aired on the Nickelodeon network and starred Larisa Oleynik. Larisa played Alex, a junior high school girl who gets strange powers after being exposed to dangerous chemicals. Jessica played a snobby rich girl who is Alex's enemy. The show was very successful. It led to bigger roles for Jessica.

Determination

In 1995, Jessica was cast as Maya Graham on the new TV series "Flipper." The series was based on the 1960s movies and TV show about a dolphin named Flipper. There was one catch to Jessica's good luck. She would have to move to Australia to film "Flipper."

Jessica spent most of the next two years working on the series. Her mother lived with her in Australia. Still, it was hard for Jessica. She told the *Toronto Sun*, "I really missed my family." The series was a great experience for Jessica. She acted, swam, and played with dolphins. She also learned how to scuba dive. She even became certified as a scuba diver by the Professional Association of Diving Instructors.

In 1996, Jessica found time in her schedule for another acting project. She filmed an "ABC Afterschool Special" called *Too Soon for Jeff*. Jessica played a high school student who becomes pregnant. Freddie Prinze Jr. played

the teenage father of her child. Freddie would later star in the movie *She's All That.*

In 1997, Jessica finished filming the second season of "Flipper." She returned home to the United States. Later that year, she landed roles on the TV shows "Beverly Hills 90210" and "Brooklyn South."

Although Jessica played high school students on TV, she didn't actually go to high school. Because she was usually working on location, she had to study with tutors. Jessica finished high school in two years instead of three.

Jessica continued to study acting. She spent a summer in Vermont studying with the Atlantic Theater Company. Playwright David Mamet and actor William H. Macy led the company and worked with the students. Mamet is known for writing many plays and screenplays, including *Glengarry Glen Ross.*

Jessica and her co-star, Peyton Haas, make a splash in "Flipper."

He helped write the screenplay for *Hannibal*, which was the sequel to *The Silence of the Lambs*. Macy has appeared in many movies including *Fargo* and *Jurassic Park III*. Jessica was the youngest student in the class, but she was a hard worker. "I was just there trying to become good at what I do," she told the British newspaper *The Sunday Times*.

WORKING WITH DREW

Jessica continued to get a steady stream of work. Each role she earned was bigger and better than the one before it. In 1998, she was in the movie *P.U.N.K.S.* She played a teenage tomboy. Later in the year, she appeared in the film *Idle Hands*, a teen horror-comedy. It was about a young man, Anton, whose hand becomes possessed. His hand forces him to kill people. Anton was played by Devon Sawa (*Wild America*). The film co-starred Seth

Jessica (far right) co-starred in the teen
horror-comedy *Idle Hands*.

Green ("Buffy the Vampire Slayer"). Seth is
also known for playing Dr. Evil's son in the
Austin Powers films. Jessica played Anton's girl-
friend, Molly. She was very excited about her
part. "I play a cool girl called Molly who rides a
motorcycle, plays bass guitar, and writes her
own music," Jessica told *The Sunday Times*.

Jessica learned a lot from working with
Drew Barrymore (above) on *Never Been Kissed*.

Jessica's next role was even better. It was in the movie *Never Been Kissed*. The movie was about Josie, a grown-up geek who goes back to high school as an undercover reporter. Jessica played one of the popular girls who makes fun of Josie. Drew Barrymore starred as Josie and also produced the movie. Jessica learned a lot from working with her. "Drew has control over her career while remaining a real sweetie," Jessica told *The Sunday Times*.

Determination

After *Never Been Kissed*, Jessica was offered many scripts. They were all for movies aimed at a teenage audience. She didn't rush to take another project. She told *The New York Times Magazine*, "I'm so lucky that [teen actors] are in demand. But I don't really want to be part of that [teen movie craze]. People blow up, and you're so overexposed, and then what do you do? I am young and I don't need to compromise. So I didn't work for eight months, which is the longest I've ever gone. I just had the faith that I was waiting for something really great." Jessica's patience paid off in a big way.

A TITANIC OFFER

After taking some time to choose her next project, Jessica was offered two great roles. The first offer was for a movie called *Paranoid*. The director was John Duigan. Duigan had directed *Sirens* and *Flirting*. *Sirens* starred Elle

MacPherson. *Flirting* starred Nicole Kidman. In *Paranoid*, Jessica played a young model named Chloe. Everyone thought that the movie would be a success, but critics did not give *Paranoid* good reviews.

However, Jessica's second offer turned out to be the best thing to happen to her career. She was given the lead role in a new television series. Jessica was chosen over one thousand other actresses who had auditioned for the part! James Cameron, the director of the blockbusters *Titanic, Terminator, Terminator 2*, and *Aliens*, created the TV series. The series would be called "Dark Angel."

It was the big break Jessica had been working so hard for.

James Cameron, seen here receiving a Filmmaker of the Year Award, developed the idea for the "Dark Angel" TV series.

CHAPTER TWO

Breakthrough

"The show has changed my life. I get to go to work every day and do something I've been working toward my whole life."

—Jessica in *Entertainment Weekly*

James Cameron created "Dark Angel" for Twentieth Century Fox. Fox was the movie studio that produced *Titanic*, which was a very expensive movie to make. The studio gave Cameron the money he needed to finish *Titanic*. In return, Cameron agreed to create and produce a TV series for Fox.

Cameron worked with another producer, Charles Eglee, to create "Dark Angel." Eglee

Jessica's sassy attitude appealed to producer James Cameron.

had produced the hit TV series "Moonlighting," which starred Cybill Shepherd and Bruce Willis. "Moonlighting" ran from 1985 to 1989. Cameron and Eglee developed a thrilling, futuristic storyline for "Dark Angel."

DARK FUTURE

"Dark Angel" is set in Seattle, Washington, in the year 2019. A stock market crash and a nuclear explosion have made life rough in the United States. Jessica plays Max. Max has been turned into a superwoman by a government experiment called Project Manticore.

The government's goal is to create perfect soldiers. Scientists altered Max's genetic make-up by adding feline DNA. This gives her cat-like speed and incredible vision. She has a photographic memory and can stay awake for long periods of time, too.

As a child, Max escaped with other genetically-

Jessica (second from right) appears with some of her "Dark Angel" co-stars: Valarie Rae Miller, Michael Weatherly, and Alimi Ballard.

enhanced children from the government lab that created them. Since then, she has struggled to keep ahead of the government forces out to kill her. The government agents are led by a Project Manticore scientist named Lydecker. Lydecker is played by John Savage.

Max works as a messenger to earn money. She also searches the Pacific Northwest for the other people who escaped the lab when she did. At the same time, she becomes involved with a cyberjournalist named Logan Cale.

Jessica's mix of intelligence, talent, and beauty was just what the producers wanted for the character of Max.

Logan is played by Michael Weatherly. Logan encourages Max to use her powers for good.

FUTURE BEAUTY

Finding the right actor to play Max was the most important and difficult part of creating "Dark Angel." The producers wanted a talented actor who was beautiful and smart. She also needed to be athletic. Whoever got the role of

Max would be expected to perform dangerous stunts. The producers also wanted someone with a multiethnic background because Max's background is mixed.

The producers knew "Dark Angel" would be compared to "Buffy the Vampire Slayer" and "The X-Files." It was important to find an actor who would help the show create its own identity. They needed someone with the potential to capture the public's imagination.

Cameron and Eglee auditioned actresses from all over the world. At first, James Cameron wasn't very impressed with Jessica. He told *Entertainment Weekly*, "She didn't look that beautiful to me when I first saw her on tape. She wasn't the ravishing beauty we now know her to be. And she wasn't particularly physically fit. But there was something about her—an attitude, a sass—that made me keep thinking of her." Eventually, the producers decided that Jessica was right for the part. "We absolutely found the strongest person for this role," Eglee told *ign.com*'s Sci-Fi TV 2000.

SUPERHUMAN TRAINING

Once Jessica won the role of Max, she had to prepare for it. Getting into shape to play a superhuman woman was quite challenging. Jessica had to work out several hours a day. She pushed herself to her limits. "I did weight training and cardio training three hours a day, gymnastics an hour and a half three days a week, and motorcycle and kung-fu training two days a week.

Did you know?

Jessica made quite an impression on her producers. They used her way of talking and her attitude to develop the character of Max.

Getting in shape for "Dark Angel" gave
Jessica plenty to smile about.

Suddenly, I had shoulders," she told
Entertainment Weekly.

Thanks to the training, Jessica is able to do
most of her own stunts. Stuntwomen are used
only for truly life-threatening stunts, like falling
from great heights.

EXPENSIVE RISK

"Dark Angel" is a high-tech TV series. It features many different special effects and stunts. This makes it a very expensive show to produce. The first episode of the series was a two-hour special. It cost more than ten million dollars to make! Each weekly one-hour episode costs about three million dollars to make. The show is filmed in Vancouver, Canada.

The producers believe that the large amount of money spent is partly responsible for its success. More than seventeen million people watched the first episode of "Dark Angel" when it premiered, or first aired, on Fox. The first episode got great reviews from critics. Many viewers and critics loved the special effects. "This is by far the most polished effort at a futuristic series ever made for television," wrote a critic for the *Miami Herald*. Jessica's performance got rave reviews as well. A critic

Jessica and James Cameron were thrilled by the rave reviews that "Dark Angel" received after its premiere.

for *The Washington Post* wrote, "She makes Max formidable, fearless, ultra-super-cool, and yet gives her depth." Support from fans made the first season a hit. The show was renewed for the 2001–02 TV season. Jessica was now the star of a hit TV series.

CHAPTER THREE

Stardom and Romance

"Michael was able to meet her energy and have a twinkle in his eye. There was an immediate chemistry between them."

—James Cameron speaking to *E! Online* about Jessica and her co-star Michael Weatherly

FRANTIC FANS

Once "Dark Angel" aired, people started talking about Jessica. They wanted to know all about her. Her celebrity status brought her many new fans. All the attention from her fans

"Dark Angel" made Jessica the one person everyone wanted to meet.

was exciting, though a bit scary. "It can get a little weird sometimes," she told *Entertainment Weekly*.

There were Web sites devoted to Jessica before "Dark Angel" aired, but after her debut as Max, she became even more popular. Jessica began to appear on the covers of dozens of magazines. She did many interviews for TV shows, newspapers, and magazines.

Fans began to recognize her everywhere she went. They asked for her autograph. When people saw her driving her car, they tried to get her to pull over and talk to them. Jessica did her best to connect with her fans. She even appeared on the official "Dark Angel" Web site. There, she competed with fans in trivia contests about the series.

Jessica never let the attention go to her head, though. She realized that her sudden fame might not last forever. Jessica told *ign.com*'s

Sci-Fi TV 2000, "It's like when someone gets sick of me, I'm out of work. So I'm just taking it how it comes right now."

BEAUTIFUL STAR

Fans weren't the only ones who wanted to meet Jessica. Suddenly, fashion designers wanted Jessica to wear their clothes. At the People's Choice Awards in 2001, Jessica wore a beautiful Dolce & Gabbana floral-print gown. "Dark Angel" won the People's Choice Award for Favorite New Television Drama. Jessica looked like a star the night "Dark Angel" won its first major TV award! Jessica was nominated for a Golden Globe Award for Best Actress in a

Jessica wore this dazzling Dolce & Gabbana gown to the People's Choice Awards.

33

Jessica's celebrity status gets her invited to many Hollywood events. Here she attends the premiere of *Apt Pupil*.

Drama Series. She wore a Marc Jacobs dress to the show.

Jessica also made a deal to promote hair-care products. She is a model for L'Oréal's Feria hair color. The color she models is called Cinnamon. Jessica is in good company. Halle Berry and Jennifer Lopez have also been L'Oréal models.

Jessica's life was getting busier with so many different people trying to get her attention. She did all she could to keep her focus on her work. "If I'm going to be in this forever, I don't need to blow up now," she told *The New York Times Magazine*.

LOVE AT LAST

As a busy nineteen-year-old television star, Jessica didn't have much time for dating. Still, rumors of romance began to spread. The most common rumor was that Jessica was involved with her co-star, Michael Weatherly.

Michael is twelve years older than Jessica. Before "Dark Angel," he appeared on the soap opera "Loving." More recently, he played Christina Applegate's ex-husband on the TV series "Jessie." He has also appeared in a number of movies including *Gun Shy* and *The Specials*. When he was in his twenties, Michael married one of his "Loving" co-stars, Amelia Heinle. They have a son, August. Amelia and Michael are now divorced.

Jessica found true love with her "Dark Angel" co-star
Michael Weatherly.

During the first season of "Dark Angel," Max and Logan's friendship deepened and became more romantic. In real life, both Jessica and Michael denied rumors of a romance.

Then the truth came out. In May 2001, Jessica and Michael announced their engagement.

The producers of the series were very supportive. The fans were also happy for Jessica and Michael. Now everyone knew why there was so much onscreen chemistry—the stars were very much in love.

WHAT'S NEXT?

Jessica's career is at a high point. As the star of a popular TV series, she's been offered many movie roles. Jessica accepted a part in the movie

Did you know?

Jessica was honored as the Breakthrough Actress of the Year at the 2001 American Latino Media Arts (ALMA) Awards.

The Sleeping Dictionary. Jessica plays a young Malaysian girl in the film. Her character's name is Selima. The movie was filmed in Malaysia, which is a country in Southeast Asia. *The Sleeping Dictionary* is the story of a

Jessica has a lot to smile about. With her talent and hard work, she has a bright future in Hollywood.

romance between Selima and a British officer in the 1930s. Roles like this are making Jessica a better actor.

Stardom and Romance

No matter what other roles she may take, Jessica still loves playing Max. "It's excellent that Max is young and a girl, and she's not apologizing for who she is," Jessica told *TV Guide Online.* "You don't find very many leading characters that have such strong opinions about things and go for it; I think people relate to her. I think she might inspire people to find their individuality."

Jessica is under contract to the show's producers for five years. So, as long as the show stays popular, we are sure to see Jessica on TV for a long time to come.

As all of her fans know, Jessica is talented and hardworking. She is sure to be a success in anything she chooses to do!

TIMELINE

1981 • Jessica Marie Alba is born on April 28 in Pomona, California.

1993 • Jessica wins the grand prize in an acting competition in Beverly Hills, California.

1994 • Jessica co-stars with Larisa Oleynik in "The Secret World of Alex Mack" on Nickelodeon.
• Jessica's first film, *Camp Nowhere,* is released.

1995 • Jessica begins her two-year run on the TV series "Flipper," filmed in Australia.

1996 • Jessica plays a pregnant teen opposite Freddie Prinze Jr. in *Too Soon for Jeff,* an "ABC Afterschool Special."

1998 • Jessica plays a tomboy in *P.U.N.K.S.*

TIMELINE

1999
- Jessica appears in *Idle Hands* with Devon Sawa and Seth Green.
- Jessica co-stars with Drew Barrymore in *Never Been Kissed*.
- Jessica appears in *Paranoid*.

2000
- Jessica is picked as one of the "Hottest 25 Stars Under 25" by *Teen People* magazine.
- Jessica is cast as Max on "Dark Angel."
- "Dark Angel" premieres on Fox on October 3.
- Jessica is nominated for a Golden Globe Award for her work on "Dark Angel."

2001
- Jessica plays Selima, a Malaysian girl, in the movie *The Sleeping Dictionary*.
- Jessica gets engaged to her "Dark Angel" co-star Michael Weatherly.
- The second season of "Dark Angel" begins in the fall.

FACT SHEET

Name	Jessica Marie Alba
Born	April 28, 1981
Birthplace	Pomona, California
Family	Father: Mark; Mother: Cathy; Brother: Josh
Sign	Taurus
Height	5'6"
Hair	Light brown
Eyes	Brown

Favorites

Actor	Drew Barrymore
Food	Mexican
Movie	*Shakespeare in Love*
Sports	Baseball, soccer, softball, scuba diving
Music	Jazz, blues, hip-hop, jungle, anything with a dance beat

NEW WORDS

agent a person who finds roles for actors, models, and musicians

audition a tryout performance

critic a person who reviews performances or works of art

director the person who has artistic control of a film or TV show

DNA deoxyribonucleic acid; a substance found in genes

feline resembling a cat

futuristic having to do with the future

genetic having to do with genes, DNA, and heredity

multiethnic having a background of mixed race, nationality, or religion

producer the person who supervises and raises money for a film or TV series

review a critic's opinion of a performance or work of art

scuba dive to swim underwater using an air tank to breathe

season a specific part of the year when a TV series airs

FOR FURTHER READING

MAGAZINES

Starlog
475 Park Avenue South
New York, NY 10016
www.starlog.com

Cinescape
12456 Ventura Blvd., Suite 2
Studio City, CA 91604
www.cinescape.com

RESOURCES

WEB SITES
The Official "Dark Angel" Web Site
www.darkangeltheseries.com
This is the official Web site for Jessica's hit TV show "Dark Angel." Among its many features are cast and crew bios, character bios, an episode guide, and a photo gallery.

Internet Movie Database: Jessica Alba
http://us.imdb.com/Name?Alba,+Jessica
Check out Jessica Alba's Internet Movie Database page. You will find information on all of her television and movie roles.

RESOURCES

You can write to Jessica at:
Jessica Alba
c/o Tribune Entertainment
TEC Building, 3rd floor
5800 Sunset Boulevard
Los Angeles, CA 90028

INDEX

INDEX

About the Author

Ursula Rivera was born and raised in
New York City. She has been writing
about celebrities for the last three years.